# This Book Belongs To:

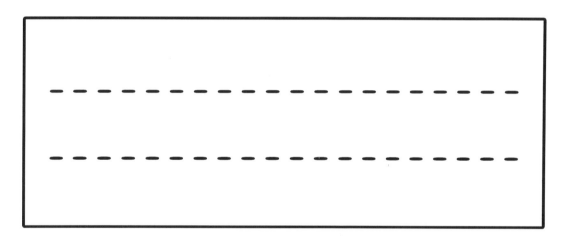

# Thank You for Choosing This Book!

Your support means everything to me, and I hope this book brings extra fun to your Halloween!

## Want More Fun & Free Resources?

Unlock **10 FREE & Unique** Pumpkin Stencils and early access to new books and special deals!
Simply scan this QR code:

## Discover More Exciting Titles!

Check out my Amazon store for more books your kids will love. Just scan the QR code or visit:

**Amazon.com/stores/author/B0CPYL9TZB**

## Share Your Experience!

Leaving a quick review helps other parents find this book. Here's how to do it in 30 seconds:

1. **Open your camera app.**
2. **Point it at the QR code on the right.**
3. **Boom!** The review page opens instantly!

Thanks for being awesome and supporting a small indie publisher like me! Your feedback makes a huge difference and helps me create more amazing books for you.

# How to Use Pumpkin Stencils?

Carving Pumpkins is a great project for adults to do with children. Kids can design the Jack-o'-lantern face, and adults can do the carving! Here are some tips to get you started:

## Pumpkin Carving Tips:

Place the pumpkin on newspaper for easy cleanup.

Cut a circle around the stem with a knife; angle the cut to prevent the top from falling in.

Find the smoothest side of the pumpkin for your design.

Cut out your stencil and tape it to the pumpkin.

Tape the stencil securely to the pumpkin,

ensuring it lies flat.

Use a large nail to punch through the stencil into the pumpkin flesh.

Cut along the scored lines with a serrated knife.

Push out the pieces from inside.

Congratulations! You have now mastered how to use pumpkin stencils.

## Share Your Experience!

Leaving a quick review helps other parents find this book. When you leave feedback, feel free to share pictures of your unique pumpkin carvings. Here's how to do it in 30 seconds:

1. Open your camera app.
2. Point it at the QR code on the right.
3. Boom! The review page opens instantly!

# Thank You for Reading!

I want to personally thank you for choosing this book and supporting my work. Your purchase means the world to me, and I truly hope this book brought joy and creativity to your Halloween season!

To show my appreciation, I'd like to offer you something special:

## Unlock Exclusive Discounts & Special Offers!

As a thank you for being an awesome reader, I'm offering exclusive discounts on my best-selling books!

Just sign up for my email list to unlock:

- **20% off** your next book purchase
- **Early access** to new releases
- **Special offers** and promotions just for subscribers

To claim your discount and discover more exciting reads, simply scan the QR code below:

You'll also receive **Free Bonus** content and be the first to hear about exciting new books for your family to enjoy!

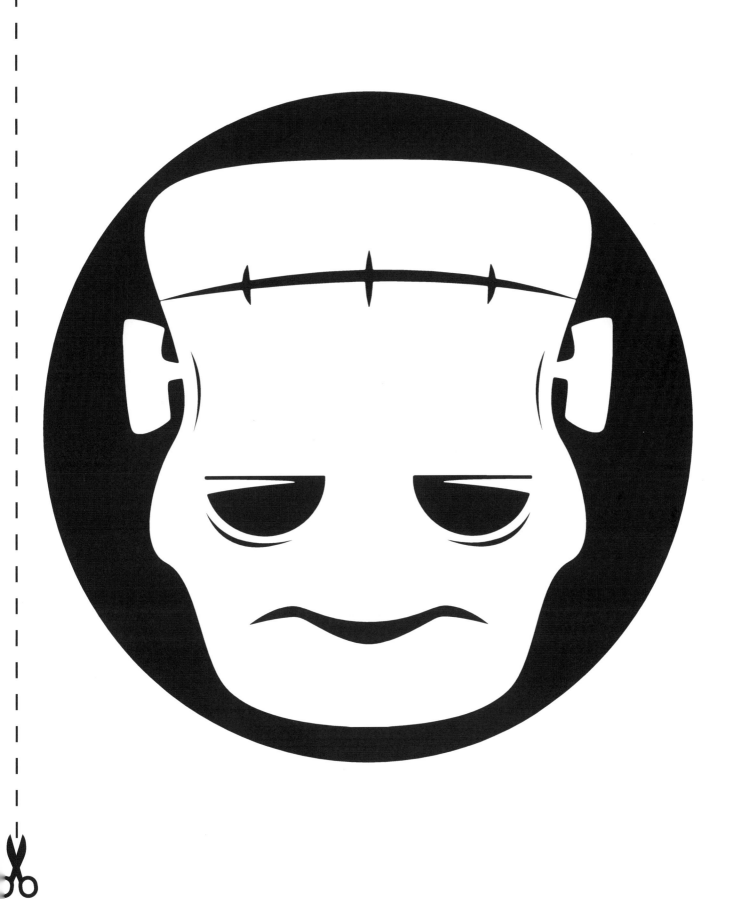

# Share With Us Your Masterpieces!

Since launching our Pumpkin Carving Stencils book, we've seen incredible creations by talented carvers like you. When you leave feedback, feel free to share pictures of your unique pumpkin carvings and celebrate your creativity with us. We're excited to see what you've carved!

## Share Your Experience!

Leaving a quick review helps other parents find this book. Here's how to do it in 30 seconds:

1. Open your camera app.
2. Point it at the QR code on the right.
3. Boom! The review page opens instantly!

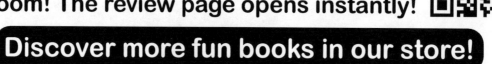

## Discover more fun books in our store!

Unlock Exclusive Discounts & Special Offers. As a thank you for being an awesome reader, I'm offering exclusive discounts on my best-selling books!

- 20% off your next book purchase
- 10 FREE & Unique Pumpkin Stencils
- Early access to new releases
- Special offers just for subscribers

To claim your discount and discover more exciting reads, simply scan the QR code above!

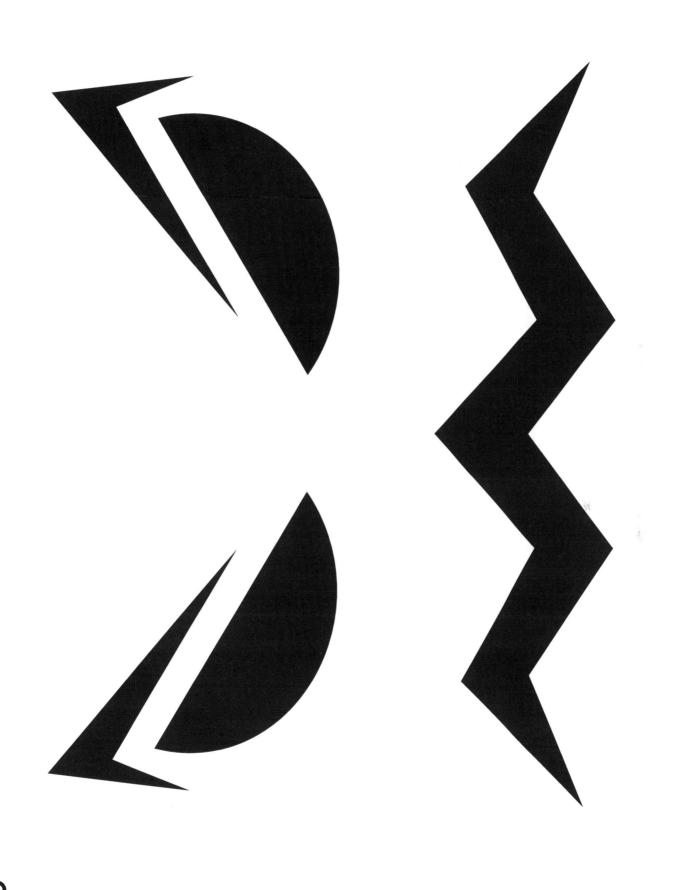

Trick or Treat

Horror Night

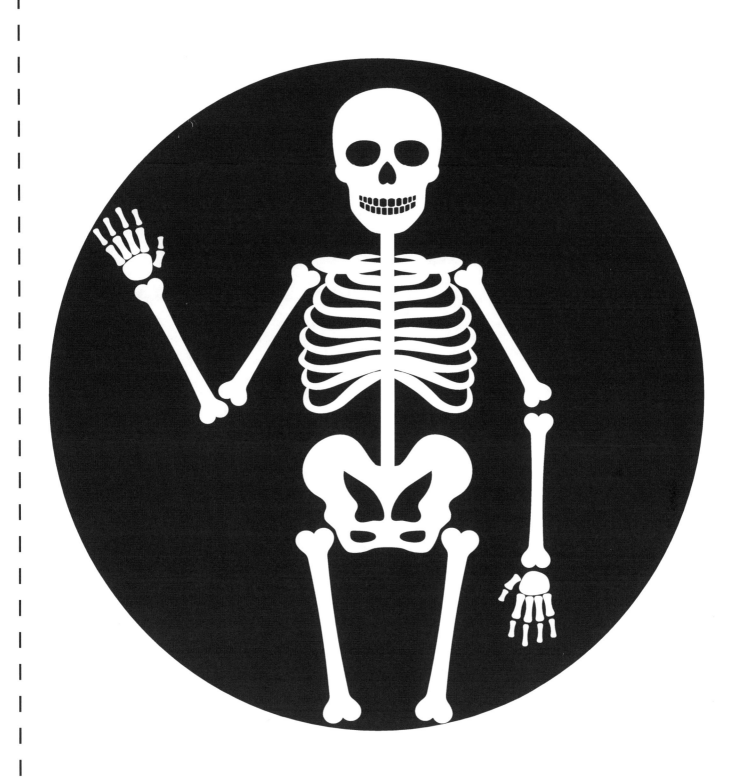

# We Appreciate You!

Thank you for using our Pumpkin Carving Stecnils book! If you enjoyed it, please leave us a review to help other parents find it.

## Discover more fun books in our store!

Unlock Exclusive Discounts & Special Offers. As a thank you for being an awesome reader, I'm offering exclusive discounts on my best-selling books!

To claim your discount and discover more exciting reads, simply scan this QR code:

- 20% off your next book purchase
- 10 FREE & Unique Pumpkin Stencils
- Early access to new releases
- Special offers and promotions just for subscribers

You'll also receive Free Bonus content and be the first to hear about exciting new books for your family to enjoy!

Have a spooktacular Halloween and enjoy your carving!

Made in the USA
Las Vegas, NV
29 October 2024

10743839R00063